The CHILDREN'S Book of EMBROIDERY

Tess Marsh

B.T. Batsford Ltd, London

To Chris Redknap

ISBN 0 7134 5142 4

Typeset by Tek-Art Ltd Kent
and printed in Great Britain by
R J Acford Ltd
Chichester, Sussex
for the publishers
B.T. Batsford Ltd
4 Fitzhardinge Street
London W1H 0AH

Contents

= Acknowledgment =

The material in this book owes its origin to Jan Beaney, who initiated the idea for an embroidery competition for local schools; the high standard of the work submitted owes much to the influence of her excellent teaching and her infectious enthusiasm for embroidery. I would like to thank her and my family for their encouragement, and also the many friends who have given me such generous help, in particular Shirley Craddock, Christine Taylor and Jane Taylor.

I am indebted to Pat Curtis and Chris Redknap for their invaluable support for the Embroidery and Textile Project, and to the children and teachers from the following schools for the examples of work:

Alexander First School, Windsor
All Saints' C.E. Junior School, Maidenhead
Alwyn Infant School, Maidenhead
Cookham Dean C.E. Primary School
Cookham Nursery School
Cookham Rise Primary School
Courthouse Primary School, Maidenhead
Cox Green Comprehensive School, Maidenhead
Fernhurst School, Maidenhead
Harmans Water Junior School, Bracknell
Holy Trinity C.E. Primary School, Cookham
Oldfield Primary School, Maidenhead
Princess Margaret Royal Free C.E. Upper School, Windsor
Royal Free C.E. Middle School, Windsor
St Mary's R.C. Primary School, Maidenhead
Swinley Primary School, Ascot
Trevelyan Middle School, Windsor
White Waltham C.E. Primary School
Windsor Girls' Upper School
Winkfield St Mary's C.E. Primary School
Woodlands Park Primary School

The Embroiderers' Guild have kindly given permission for the reproduction of photographs of two embroideries from their collection. I am also grateful to J. & P. Coats for allowing me to use some of their stitch diagrams and to the Maidenhead Teachers' Centre for the colour transparencies. My very special thanks are due to Jean Gilson for her excellent photographs, to Margaret and Charles Suckling for their constant support, to Barbara McColm for correcting the text, and to her and to my son, Dominic, for their help in mounting and finishing the diagrams.

All photographs are by Jean Gilson unless otherwise credited. All drawings are by the author unless otherwise credited.

Children of All Saints' Junior School, Maidenhead, working on pieces for the Berkshire Schools' Embroidery and Textile Project (*Photo: Maidenhead Advertiser.*)

5

Dragon against cloud symbols on a man's semi-formal coat (*ch'i-fu*) from China – late nineteenth century; embroidered in silver and gold thread on blue twilled silk using laid and couched work. (*Embroiderers' Guild Collection.*)

Introduction

There is no end to the variety of ways in which fabric and thread can be used to produce pictures, to decorate clothes and to make and decorate articles for use in the home.

Men and women have done this all over the world from the earliest times. Elaborate decoration on church vestments and on clothes showed how important, wealthy and powerful certain people in a society were.

Beautiful embroidery has also been done by very poor people, sometimes to economize, like the early settlers in America who developed patchwork in order to make use of every precious little scrap of fabric; but mostly because all people love colours and patterns, and have a need to make things individually their own, which can be done by means of decorative stitchery.

The finest example of pictorial embroidery is the Bayeux Tapestry, probably made in England in about 1070. It gives a vivid account of the events leading up to the Battle of Hastings and gory scenes from the battle itself. Embroidery does not have to be only pretty and decorative!

A floral spray on velvet worked in floss and twisted silks and applied fish scales – British, late nineteenth century. The fish scales were soaked in cold water until they were soft and pliable and two small holes were pierced near the base of each scale. (*Embroiderers' Guild Collection* .)

At the D-Day Museum in Southsea the Overlord Embroidery which was completed in 1973 is on display. This tells the story of the invasion and the battle of Normandy by the Allied forces in 1944. Khaki cloth and gold braid from the soldiers' uniforms are among the 50 materials used, as well as the whole beret of one of the paratroopers.

You can see, then, that all sorts of fabrics and threads can be used and even unusual items such as feathers, porcupine quills and fish scales have been used when other materials have not been available, or to achieve the effect required.

Ideas for designs can be taken from the most unlikely objects. Would you have thought of looking for a design in a piece of bacon?

The pictures in this book show many ideas which have been worked by children in fabric and thread.

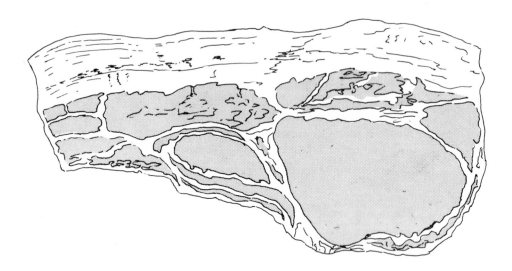

There are interesting shapes in this drawing of a bacon rasher. On the next page you can see how a section has been taken out and used as a design which makes a good repeat pattern. The outline formed by those two shapes has been simplified to make a different motif, which can also be used as a repeat pattern.

8

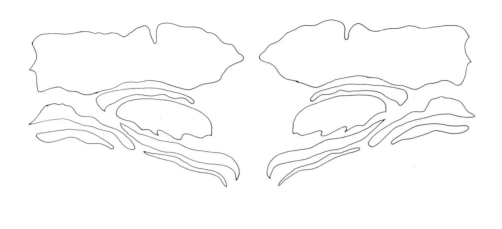

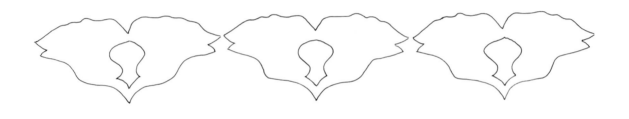

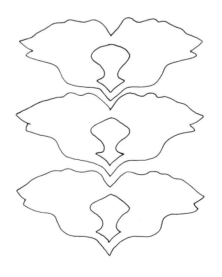

Things
══ You Will Need ══

Became a collector. Everybody likes to collect and the textile artist can have great fun collecting the following items:

Pictures and postcards

Keep a scrapbook and have separate sections for pictures of people, animals, buildings, flowers.

If you take photographs yourself you can keep a record of things from which you can get ideas for designs and colour schemes, such as the patterns of roof tiles or the colours and textures in a rough stone wall.

Sketches, rubbings and prints

Rubbings can be made from bark and other textured surfaces, and prints taken from natural or man-made objects. Even dead moths found on window-sills may have lovely designs on their wings. Keep a sketchbook to make a note of the markings. A magnifying glass may help you to see them properly.

Fabric

Collect a variety of colours and different textures: smooth, furry, rough; matt and shiny; stiff or stretchy; closely woven or very open, like rug canvas or vegetable bags; transparent fabrics such as net, chiffon or organdie.

Threads

Collect colours you specially like and store them in plastic sweet jars – all the shades of one colour in one jar. Anything from very fine embroidery threads to thick wools, ribbons, tapes, raffia and various kinds of string can be useful.

Unusual objects

Unusual items such as shells, feathers, buttons, beads and sequins are sometimes just what you need and it is worth having a small collection.

Needles

You will find the following useful:
crewel needles in various sizes for stitching with fine threads and wools;
knitters' needles and tapestry needles for working on coarse fabrics and canvas;
beading needles for beads.

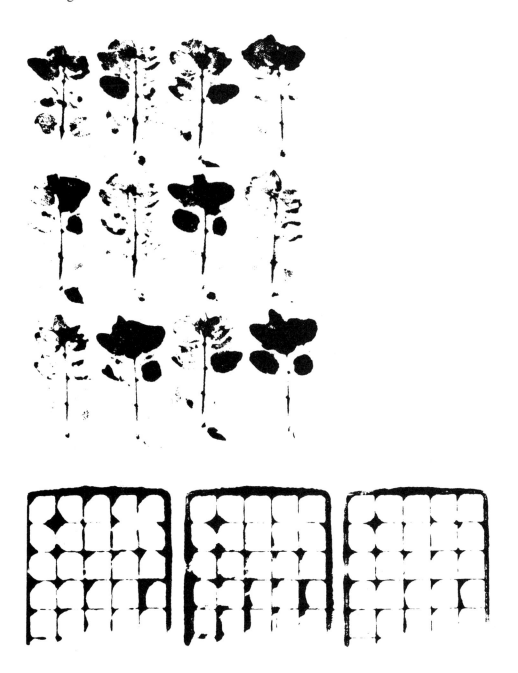

Starting Points

Ideas for embroidery designs of your own can be found almost anywhere. The colours and textures of different fabrics and threads might suggest a picture, or you might want to work out a design to fit a particular shape. Throughout the book you will find ideas for subjects for embroidery, some of which you may never have thought suitable for working in textiles. Flowers and animals have been widely used for embroidery designs in all countries in all ages, and so have very regular geometric patterns.

Fabrics: shapes, textures and colours

The shapes of pieces of fabric from your collection may look like a familiar object or suggest a scene.

Enjoy feeling the textures of fabric: what do the coarse rough surfaces remind you of, or the smooth, soft pile of velvet? And what about the delicate, transparent fabrics such as georgette, silk, net and voile?

A lot of dark colours in your collection could be used to make a night scene.

'Slide'. Matthew Greenwood (5) found a slide-shaped piece of red material which he stuck down onto a background of cream hessian. He added little felt figures of children playing on and around the slide to make a simple yet lively picture.

'Bride' by Susan Lawrie (10). The fine white net made Susan think of a wedding veil which became the focal point of her picture of the bride.

Subjects of special interest

'Concorde' by Geoffrey Henry (7). Geoffrey was working on a project on transport and decided to embroider Concorde on a piece of canvas (10 holes to 25 mm – 1 in.) in white, grey and black wools using satin stitches. By placing the aircraft at an angle he has given the feeling of it climbing steeply through the clouds.

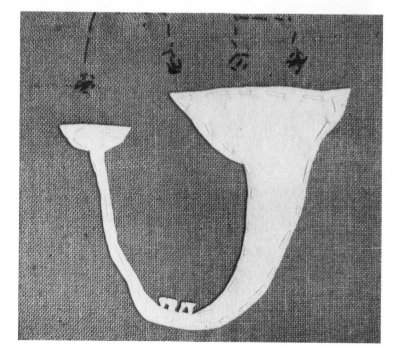

'Horn' by Neville Henry (5). Music is a subject of great interest to many people. Neville has observed the shape and smooth curves of the horn which he cut out of yellow felt and stitched to a piece of blue hessian using running stitch. The musical notes are worked in black thread in straight stitches.

School subjects and games

Every school subject is a possible source of ideas for embroidery.

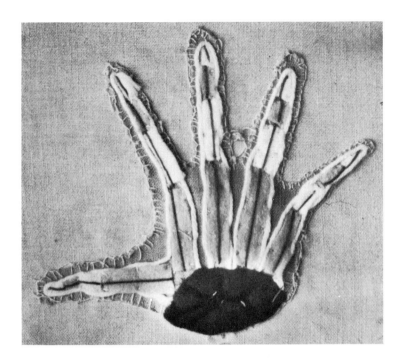

'Anatomical Hand' by Leighanne Springate (8). In a PE lesson Leighanne learnt about parts of the body on which to balance. Having made a careful study of the internal structure of the hand she cut out a hand shape in a piece of pink fabric and applied it to a background using blanket stitch. Pieces of applied pink, white and red felt and a couched white thread show the positions of the bones and the muscles, and the veins are worked in straight stitches in blood-red thread.

'Goalkeeper' by Scott Shepherd (7). Scott's favourite sport is football and you can feel this goalkeeper stretching and jumping to catch the ball. The felt goalposts and clothes are held down with stab stitches. Thick orange silk thread was used for the goal-net.

Comic-book faces and stories

The pictures in story-books and comics are often very simply drawn and easy to copy freehand and then enlarge to the size you want. This is done by dividing the small drawing into a grid of 1 cm (½ in.) squares; if you want to double the size, draw a grid of 2 cm (1 in.) squares on another sheet of paper and copy exactly what you see in each small square into the larger squares.

You can illustrate a story you have read or one you have written yourself.

'Denis the Menace' by Lindsay Hill (9). Denis the Menace is made of simple fabric shapes stitched by hand to the background hessian using buttonhole stitch. The red velvet tongue is stitched only at the top so that it is loose and flops around! This three-dimensional feature adds interest to the flat shapes.

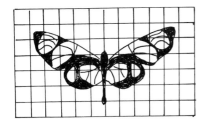

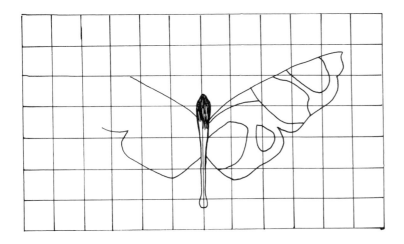

'Fairytale Princess' by Miranda Absalom (10). The white dress and the blonde hair of this princess show up well against the dark navy blue and black of the background. Can you spot all the nocturnal creatures lurking in the picture? They were copied from pictures in books before being cut out of fabric. Sequins make the owl's eyes shine.

Self-portraits and portraits of relations

'Self-portrait' by Simone Gibson (4 years 11 months). Draw a picture of yourself, at least 38 cm (15 in.) from the top of the head to the toes. Hair can be added and the figure dressed with fabric pieces in different shapes, colours and textures.

18

'Granny-on-the-sofa' by Kirsten
Perfitt (11). The wallpaper is
printed fabric; the lampstand is a
short length of French knitting;
braid has been used for the
pelmet; and the lace curtain is
arranged so that it looks as if it has
been blown into the room. The
settee, the cushion and the lamp-
shade are stuffed and Granny's
face, hands and legs are made of
tights and acrylic stuffing. The
whole effect is similar to seven-
teenth-century stumpwork.

Birds and trees

When there is a lot of detail in an object, such as the many branches and leaves of a tree, or the patterns made by the feathers of a bird, it is important to concentrate on the main shapes and use those for your design. Remember also to look at the background shapes which they form, to make sure that they are pleasing.

It is useful to cut the shapes out of paper first. Then use your paper cut-outs as templates and cut out your fabric around them.

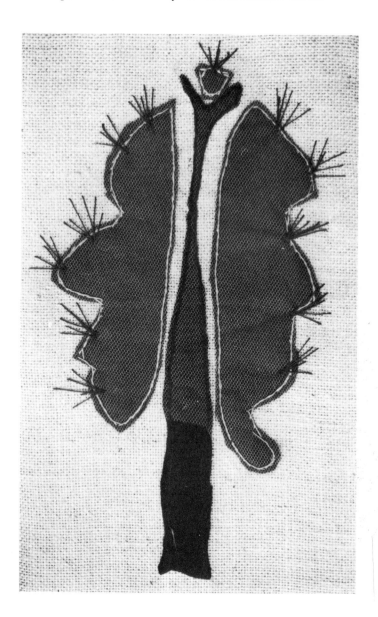

'Tree' by Joanne Cherry (10). Here the simplified shapes of the trunk and the foliage cut out of green and brown felt have been applied to a background of beige hessian. Net has been placed over the felt to give it texture and to soften the strong colours. It is held down with stem stitch. The spiky quality of the pine needles is well suggested by groups of straight stitches.

'Bird and Shadow' by Edward Brian-Davis (10). This simple bird shape, cut out of green felt, has been decorated with yellow net on the wings which are edged with herringbone stitch, and rows of chain stitch on the tail. The body is an oval shape, trapunto-stuffed. The repetition of the shape as a shadow in blue net slightly darker than the background is an interesting idea which could be developed into a repeat pattern.

Tie-dyed patterns

Tie-dyeing provides random patterns which can be used as a background for embroidery. The patterns may suggest a scene or a face. Cold-water dyes can be used with plain cotton material such as bleached calico, or even old sheets and pillowcases. New fabric must be thoroughly washed to remove all dressing. Soak old or new fabric in cold water before dyeing. The wet material can be pleated, folded, rolled and stitched, and pebbles, shells, seeds and buttons can be tied in *very* tightly. The tied fabric is left in the dye for about 20-30 minutes, then allowed to dry before it is untied.

'Two Trees and a Fence' by Michael Thompson (12). The salmon pink and mauve colours and the pattern of the tie-dyed background create an atmospheric sky onto which tree skeletons of purple felt and a grey felt fence have been applied with machine stitching.

Bark rubbings

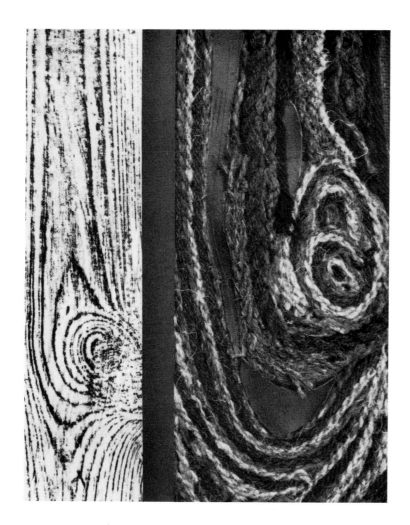

'Bark Rubbing' by Ronan Guillou (11). This bark rubbing has been interpreted as a collage using wool, raffia and pieces of leather. It could also be worked in lines of stitches such as stem, raised chain band, chain stitch and couching. Good patterns for embroidery can be rubbed from frosted glass, wallpaper, floor tiles and floorboards.

Ink blots

This could be messy work so make sure that you are wearing old clothes or an apron. Work on newspaper.

Drop a blob of ink onto a sheet of non-absorbent paper and twist and tip the paper to make the ink run in various directions. Experiment until you have a satisfactory pattern. The biggest shapes can be cut out of fabric, applied and padded, and the thinner lines can be worked in stitches.

'Ink blot' by Alison Potter (13). Alison has used many different stitches to interpret the spidery lines of the ink blot: cretan stitch, chain stitch, back stitch, couching and whipped cords with clusters of French and bullion knots.

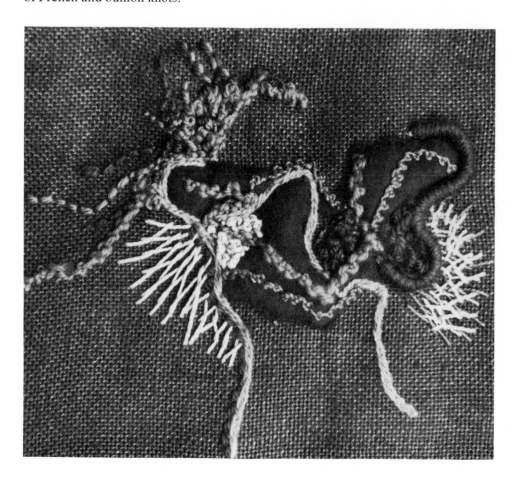

Exploded paper shapes

Circles, squares and rectangles of paper can be cut into shapes which are then 'exploded' – that is, moved away from one another. Make sure that the sizes of the shapes vary and that the spaces between them are pleasing and are also of different sizes; some should be very narrow and others wider, but none should be too wide, otherwise the design will not hold together.

An example of an exploded circle and how it can be decorated with stitching will be found in the section on Stitches, page 35.

Stitches

Stitches can be used in many ways.

Running stitch, whipped running stitch, chain stitch, raised chain band, couching and buttonhole stitch are mostly used to follow a line. They can also be used to fill in shapes within the design and can even be worked in such a way that layers of the same stitch are built up one on top of the other to give a heavy texture.

French knots, bullion knots, seeding, buttonhole rings, backstitch wheels and star stitches can provide areas of texture. If you are working a cluster of any of these stitches you can add interest by varying their size and the thickness of the threads in which they are worked and by mixing matt and shiny threads.

Satin stitch gives a lovely smooth effect and **fly stitch** makes a pretty, lacy filling.

It is worth experimenting with a stitch when you have learnt how to work it, to see what effects you can get.

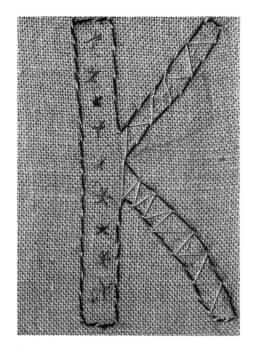

'Letter 'K'' by Karen Harnden (5). The letter 'K' has been outlined in running stitch in white thread which has been whipped with brown. A pink thread has been laced in and out of the stitches to give a zigzag effect. Star stitches decorate the upright of the letter.

Running stitch.

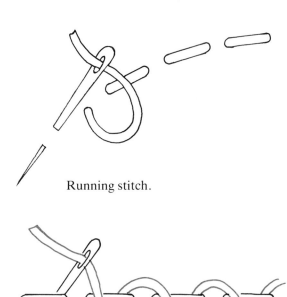

Whipped running stitch.

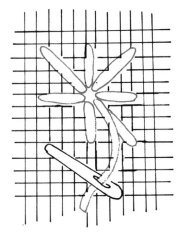

Star stitch.

'Satin Stitch Blocks' by Lucy Roberts (5). Blocks of satin stitch have been worked in red, white and blue wools on canvas (5 holes to 25 mm – 1 in.).

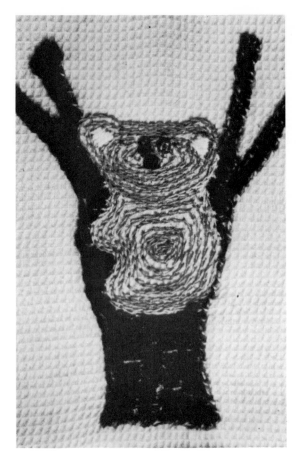

'Koala' by Alison Graham (10).
Chain stitch has been used to fill in the whole koala bear. The oval shape which the stitching follows for the head gives the bear a lovely grin. The tree is worked in vertical rows of satin stitch.

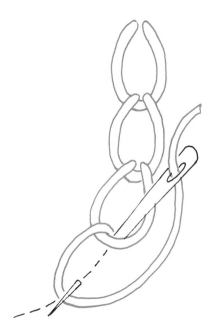

Chain stitch.

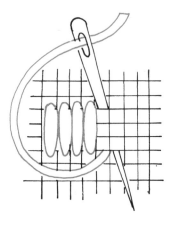

Satin stitch.

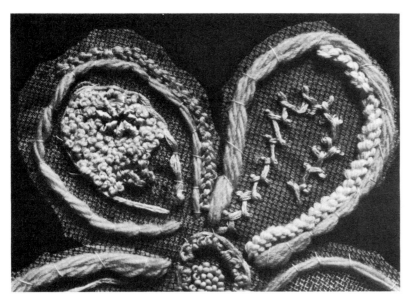

'Yellow Flower' (upper half) by Sau Ling Wong (9). The petals of this simple flower shape have been decorated with a variety of interesting stitches. In the centre of the left-hand petal a backstitch wheel in shiny thread is surrounded by French knots to give a crunchy effect. The right-hand petal is outlined with a couched thread and a line of raised chain band. There is cretan stitch in the centre.

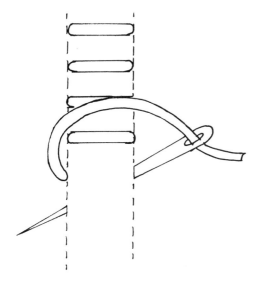

Raised chain band:
1 Work a ladder of stitches along the line of the stitching.

2 Work chain stitch over the bars without going through the fabric.

Backstitch wheel:
1 Work eight straight stitches in a star shape.

2 Bring the needle up at point A and work backstitch over the arms of the star going back over one stitch and bringing the needle under two stitches. Do not go through the fabric.

3 Backstitch wheel.

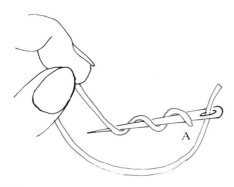

French knots:
1 Bring the thread through the fabric at A.
2 Hold the thread taut with the thumb and forefinger about 2 cm (¾ in.) from the fabric.
3 Twist the needle around the thread two or three times.

4 Still holding the thread taut, put the needle into the fabric at point B, just beside point A, and take it through to the back, making sure that the knot remains on the surface.

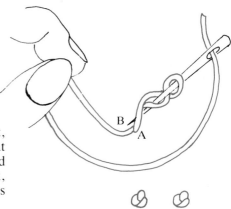

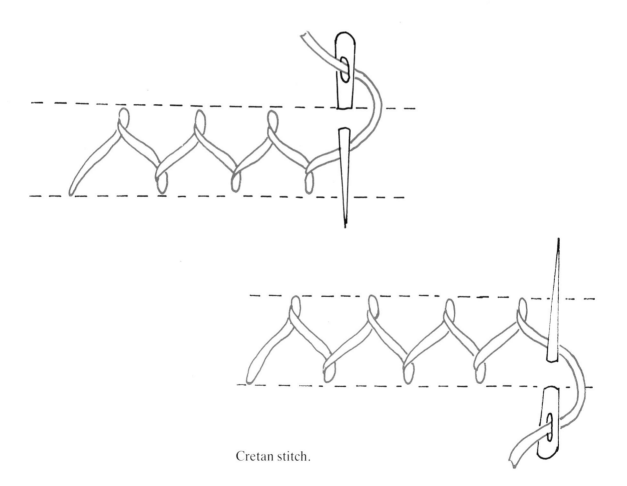

'Yellow Flower' (lower half) by Sau Ling Wong (9). The left-hand petal is decorated with cretan stitch in the centre, couching and French knots around the edge. In the right-hand petal are three buttonhole rings worked in embroidery thread, with beads and French knots added.

Cretan stitch.

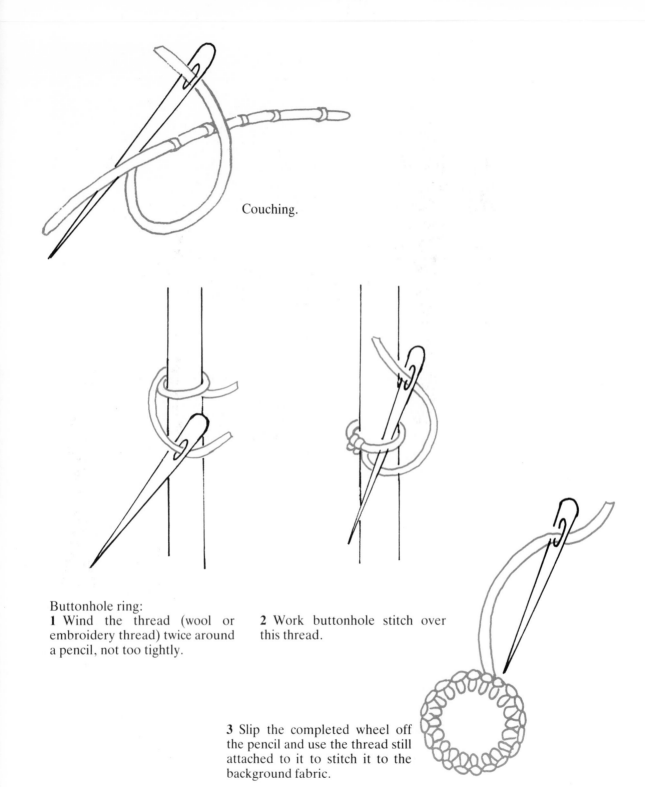

Couching.

Buttonhole ring:
1 Wind the thread (wool or embroidery thread) twice around a pencil, not too tightly.

2 Work buttonhole stitch over this thread.

3 Slip the completed wheel off the pencil and use the thread still attached to it to stitch it to the background fabric.

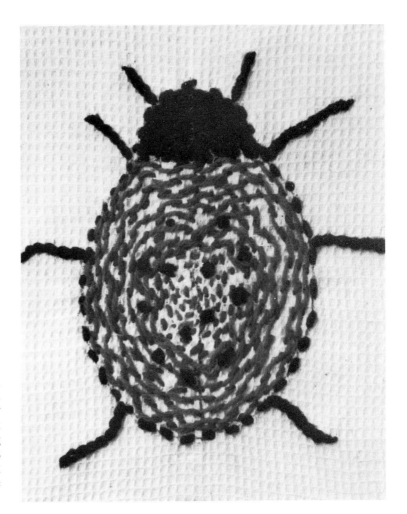

'Ladybird' by Lisa Crick (10). This ladybird is worked in concentric rows of running stitch in black wool, leaving a circular area in the middle of the back which has been filled with seeding in red. The running stitch has been laced with red, and black French knots make the spots. The legs are worked in chain stitch.

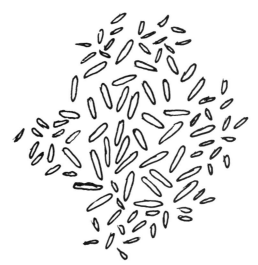

Seeding. This filling stitch is made up of small straight stitches placed in various directions, unevenly spaced.

'Flamingo' by Parmjit Kaur (10). The flamingo is outlined in stem stitch, with satin stitch giving a strong line to the neck. The blanket stitch has been used as a filling stitch, evenly spaced on the legs and neck, and varying from close to wide to shape the body. Blanket stitch is also good for applying fabrics which tend to fray. When worked very close together, it is known as buttonhole stitch.

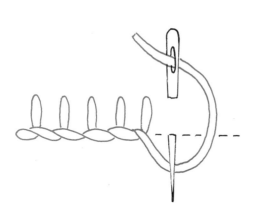

Blanket stitch.

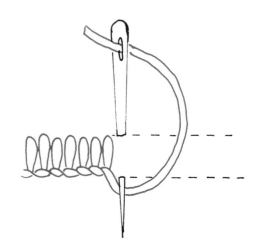

Buttonhole stitch.

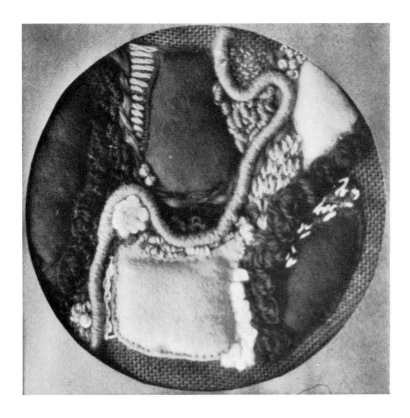

'Exploded Circle' by Julia Crowe (13). The spaces between the trapunto-padded felt shapes of this exploded circle are decorated with stitches to give a contrast between plain areas and textured areas. Fly stitch and bullion knots are among the stitches used to fill in the spaces.

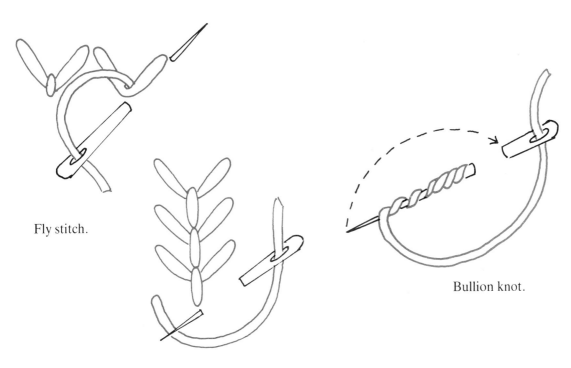

Fly stitch.

Bullion knot.

35

Detail from 'Willow Cottage' by Sarah Crisp (10). The detail of the willow tree shows how the willow branches are well suggested by stem stitch, and the straight stitches form the leaves. Blanket stitch has been used to apply the tree trunk. Herringbone stitch is also a good stitch to use for appliqué.

Stem stitch.

Herringbone stitch.

Techniques

Apart from stitching, there are many embroidery techniques which can be used.

One of the simplest and the one which gives very quick results is **appliqué**. A shape is cut from a piece of fabric and applied to a background fabric by machine using the zigzag stitch, or by hand using blanket stitch or herringbone stitch, which neaten the edges of the fabric being applied. Nets and leathers are caught down with stab stitches. When stitching leather, always push the needle down into the leather from above.

Canvas work is a counted-thread technique which is usually worked in formal patterns but can be worked freely.

Drawn-thread work gives an open, lacy effect.

These are some of the techniques which can be worked successfully even by beginners, but there are many more which you can learn about from embroidery books. When you have an idea for a design or a picture, consider carefully which technique and which stitches will enable you to interpret it most satisfactorily.

Appliqué

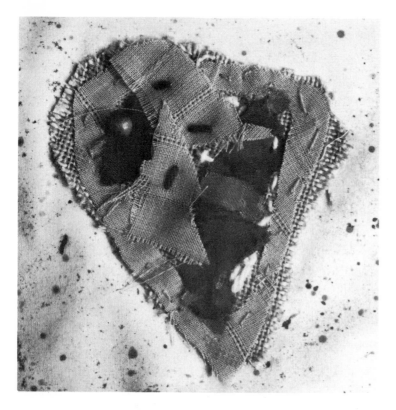

'Fish' by Melanie White (7). Pieces of fabric have been selected for their colours (pale apricot and purple) and for their shapes, and applied freely to the marbled background fabric, over-lapping and lying one on top of the other to give a scaly effect. They have been stitched down with running stitch.

'Church'. Group work (9-11) by All Saints' Junior School, Maidenhead. The main shapes of the building, the trees and the clouds have been held down with blanket stitch. Care has been taken to match the warp and the weft of the applied pieces with that of the background fabric to prevent puckering.

Canvas work

'Rooftops'. Group work (11-13) by Fernhurst School. These rooftops were worked in separate sections by several girls. Here are some of the canvas stitches they used, working on canvas 12 holes to 25 mm (1 in.).

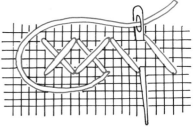

Cross stitch.

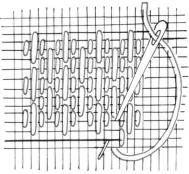

Hungarian stitch.

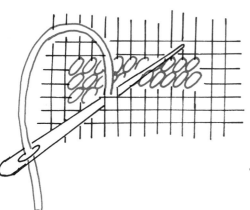

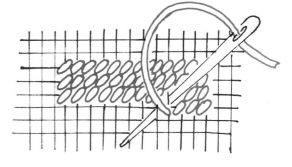

Tent stitch.

Darning

Darning can be worked on many fabrics from fine linen to coarse hessian, and also on other less conventional materials such as net, scrim, vegetable bags and curtain net. The thread you use will depend on the size of the holes: on very coarse weaves ribbons and strips of fabric can be used. The darning can be done in a regular pattern or at random to give textured effects.

Photograph of a coastal scene.

'Darning' by Victoria Clisby (13). This example of darning shows how a photograph can be used as the basis of an abstract design. The main areas of light and dark have been copied from the photograph to make an original embroidery design.

Drawn thread

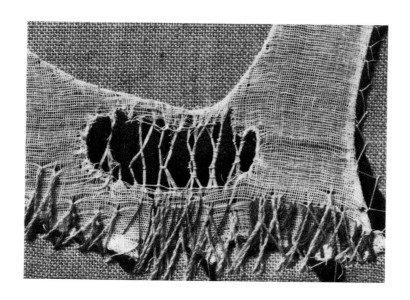

'Tree Trunk' by Leslie Borrill (10). To suggest the hollow in this tree trunk Leslie has drawn out some of the weft threads in the white scrim, leaving the warp threads which have been grouped together with free needleweaving. The picture is mounted on black card so that the hollow looks deep, with strands of plants or spiders' webs stretched across it.

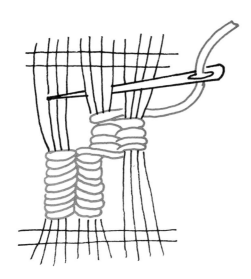

Needleweaving.

Felt sculpture

The main advantages of felt are that it does not fray and can be easily cut into shapes and manipulated. Cut-off scraps can be built up in many different ways to give a three-dimensional effect. You can experiment by rolling long strips, plaiting, stacking and gathering them to see what sort of textures you can produce.

'Abstract' by Nicholas Udall (9). Squares of different colours have been stacked on top of one another. Red, green, white, yellow and shocking pink felt have been used.

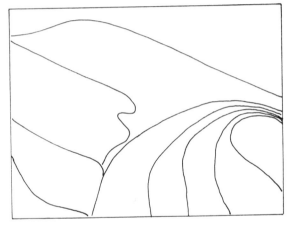

'Contours'. Group work (11-13) by Princess Margaret Royal Free Upper School. Using only purple felt, the free interpretation of these lines from a contour map concentrates for effect on the textures and the trapunto padding. (See page 44.)

Trapunto

Trapunto is a useful technique for getting a subtle raised effect in a particular area of your embroidery.

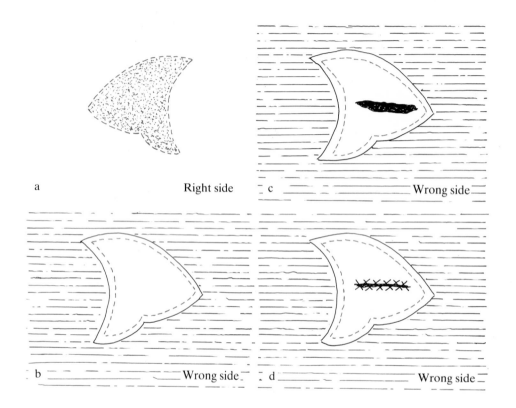

a   Right side   c   Wrong side

b   Wrong side   d   Wrong side

Either:
a Apply the shape to be padded to the right side using blanket stitch, buttonhole stitch, herringbone stitch, or machine zigzag stitching.
Or:
b Cut out of calico the shape to be padded, making it 1 cm bigger all round and apply it to the wrong side of the background fabric with backstitch or machine straight stitch, so that the outline of the shape shows only as stitching on the right side.
c Carefully cut a slit in the backmost piece of fabric only, and push stuffing between the two layers.
d When the shape is stuffed sufficiently to give the effect you want, stitch up the slit with herringbone stitch or oversewing.

44

Creatures
Great and Small

All shapes and sizes of animals, birds, fishes and insects have been widely used in embroidery. The Elizabethan embroiderers used to fill any spaces left on the embroidered fabric with bees, flies, caterpillars and butterflies.

Many creatures have beautiful markings from which designs can be taken. Interesting repeat patterns can be made out of the whole shapes of creatures or a part of them, such as the heads or even just the eyes. If you are making a repeat pattern, look carefully at the background shapes you are making: they should be as pleasing as the main shapes.

'Spider' by Adam Brookman (9). Metal thread for the web and a textured thread for the spider's legs are couched to the green felt background. Chain stitch stripes have been worked onto the spider's body which is cut out of light brown felt, applied with blanket stitch and trapunto-padded. Fabric paints have been used to give a foliage effect in the top right- and bottom left-hand corners of the picture.

45

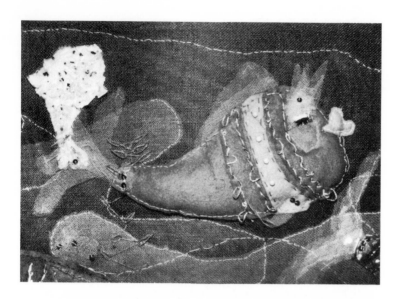

'Fish'. Group work (9-11) by Harmans Water Junior School. This purple fish was decorated with strips of blue and yellow felt, whipped running stitch and beads and then applied to the background hessian before being stuffed. The fins, the 'eyebrows' and the tail are made of pale blue and white nets. The large net shapes behind and below the fish suggest the water, and the 'seaweed' near the tail is worked in detached chain stitches.

'Tiger' by Karen Fletcher (11). The tiger's head was drawn onto the cream hessian and is worked entirely in straight stitches to create the furry, textured effect.

'Owl' by Timothy Nicholson (10). Fabric feathers in cotton and hessian are stitched to a velvet background with long straight stitches. Only a few feathers have been used to make a decorative pattern. The owl's head is made from a coarse scrim pulled into holes and frayed at the edges. The leather eyes have been glued down. Knitting wools and textured threads have been couched down to form the body and feet and to encircle the eyes. The beak is stitched in wool, and straight stitches fill in the body shape. (*Photograph: Roger Cuthbert.*)

Colour

Colour is always an important consideration, whether you are choosing clothes, decorating a room, painting a picture or designing an embroidery. Here are some questions to ask yourself when you are deciding what colours to use:

1 What colours do I like?
Each person has an individual taste in colours. It is important to enjoy the colours you use.

2 To what use is the embroidery going to be put?
If you are making a large panel which must be seen from a distance you will want to use colours which give strong contrast of tone, such as yellow and purple.

3 What effect do I want my embroidery to have?
Colours have different effects on people. Blue and green are soothing; red and yellow are exciting.

4 Is the texture of stitching and the fabric more important than variety of colour?
Many embroidery techniques are traditionally worked in one colour only because the effect aimed for is created by texture or the play of light and shade. The stitching of the 'Ink blot' (page 24) is worked only in shades of mauve and the felt sculpture 'Contours' (page 43) is done in one colour.

Primary colours

The primary colours are red, blue and yellow. All other colours are made by mixing two of them or all three of them together.

Secondary colours

Secondary colours are those made by mixing any two primaries:

>   yellow + red = orange
>   yellow + blue = green
>   blue + red = purple

'Aces and Spades' by *All Saints' Junior School. Sarah Cox (9)*. The use of primary colours produces a very bright and striking piece of work. The addition of black, white and bottle green makes the primary colours seem even more vivid.

'Salad Roll' by *Mary Moss (10)*. This salad roll is made of a simple shape cut from calico and trapunto-padded. Pieces of tomato and cucumber are cut from felt on which pips are embroidered. The slices of egg are made of string, and scraps of knitting are used as lettuce. The 'roll' is mounted on a section of red plastic plate. The turquoise background card is an effective foil for the red plate.

'Pot Plant in a Window' by *Lee Katrina Gray (12)*. This picture has been made most attractive by the use of complementary colours – green chain stitch for the foliage and red fabric for the flowers and flower pot. The cold and warm colours (blue and red) contrast effectively, as do the large, plain areas of the trapunto-stuffed curtains and the texture of the white net curtains, the flowers and the stitching.

'Lady in Pink Hat' by *Stephen Haylor (12)*. The hat is cut out of pink binka and applied; the crown has been padded and trimmed with a piece of cord. The hair is made of wool loosely held down with stitches to form curls. Lace has been used for the choker and the dress.

'Cock' by *Paula Morris (10)*. The fabrics available suggested this scene to Paula. In her collection were green velvet and several sky blues; gold fabric and red net made her think of a sunrise and a crowing cock. She has used couching, blanket stitch and fly stitch.

'Bowl of Fruit' by *Rebecca Hamilton (10)*. The fruit was drawn on paper, traced and transferred to fine binka with fabric dyes; certain areas were then decorated with canvas stitches.

Complementary colours

Complementary colours make striking contrasts. Each pair of complementary colours consists of the primary colour left out in the mixing of a secondary colour, and that secondary colour itself:

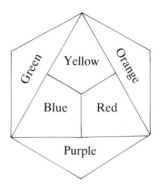

red is complementary to *green* (blue + yellow);
blue is complementary to *orange* (yellow + red);
yellow is complementary to *purple* (blue + red).

Warm colours are red, orange and yellow, the colours of fire and the sun. These are used in the foreground of a scene as they seem to come forward.

Cool colours are blue, purple and green, the colours of ice and water. These are used for distance as they appear to recede.

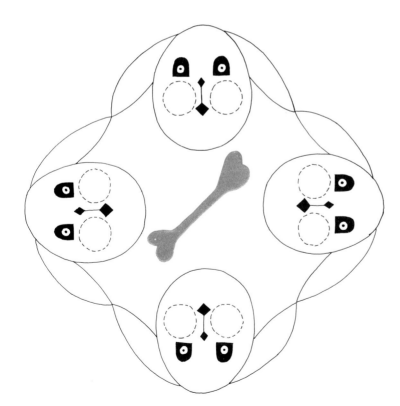

Often a small amount of red will enliven a design or picture worked mostly in cool colours or in black and white, as in this repeat pattern of a dog's head which is part of a quilt made by ten-year-old children from Cookham Rise School.

Faces and Figures

People are fascinating subjects for painting and drawing and for embroidery too. They give the opportunity for a touch of humour. It is best to work quite simply to begin with. Don't try to get an exact likeness; concentrate on the main features.

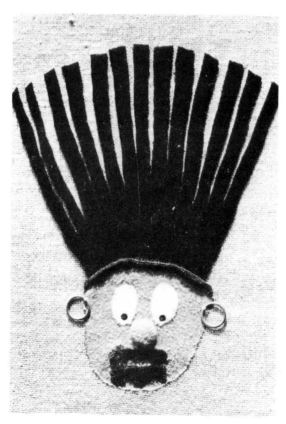

'Head' by Loredana Cofone (9). The main shape of the hair is glued to the background fabric; the face, the eyes and the nose are stitched. The nose is stuffed and the earrings are brass curtain rings.

'Tie-dyed Head' by Enzo Antinoro (9). The tie-dyed background has suggested this amusing face. The cap is a piece of cream fabric applied with running stitches trimmed with a multi-coloured pompom and streamers. The nose is a little padded patch and other features are put in with stitching.

'Granny Knitting' by Caroline Richardson (11). Satin stitch and straight stitching have been used to embroider granny, her knee rug, the cat and the chair. Real knitting and toothpick knitting needles give a three-dimensional effect.

'Clown' by Belinda Hall (9½). Belinda was fascinated by clowns and circuses. She used chain stitch and satin stitch in brightly coloured silks and lots of sequins to suggest the rich and dazzling quality of the clown's clothes.

Three-dimensional Embroidery

It is fun to make three-dimensional objects in fabric and threads or to build up a design or a picture in relief. The addition of one or more three-dimensional features such as a tongue or a nose protruding from the surface can add interest to your embroidery.

'Dragon' by Virginia Turner (18). Many preparatory drawings of reptiles were done before Virginia made this three-dimensional dragon out of calico. The scales on its body are worked in wadded quilting.

Detail from 'Faces in the Tube'. Group work (11-13) by Cox Green Comprehensive School. This crowd of people was made by a group of boys. The toe-ends of variously coloured tights were cut off and filled with acrylic wadding. When the heads had been shaped by pushing and pinching, the features were stitched into place; hollows for eye sockets were stitched from side to side across the bridge of the nose. Eyes, mouths, hair and clothes were made using beads, buttons, pieces of fabric, threads, paint and dyes. The background on which these heads are mounted was painted in with fabric dyes. Your first attempts at this technique may not be quite successful but with second and third tries you will get excellent faces which take on a personality of their own.

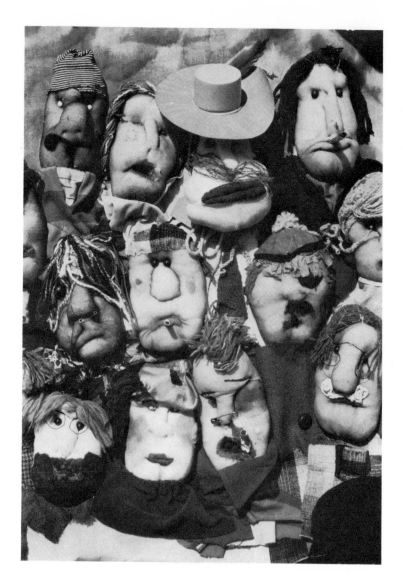

'Balloon' by Mark Coleman (9). The patchwork design of the fabric used for the balloon and the red and white gingham for the basket have been well chosen. The balloon is trapunto-quilted and the ropes are worked in back stitch. The thumb-nail sized faces of the figures are made of stuffed tights like the fist-sized heads of the tube crowd in the previous picture.

'Picnic Platter' by Carol Gillies (13). The plate, made of vilene covered with organdie, has a machine-stitched pattern around the edge. The sandwiches, slices of apple and Battenburg cake are made of felt pieces joined together with blanket stitch, and the toffees are made from foam covered with decorated organdie.

'Landscape with Stitched Fields'. Group work (11-13) by Cox Green Comprehensive School. Scrim has been ruched for the un-cultivated fields and the crops are a patchwork of embroidered sections. Lollipop stick fences, pompom bushes and a cardboard building make the miniature scene realistic.

═ Unusual Materials ═

Like collage, embroidery gives you the opportunity to be inventive and to make use of many materials besides fabric and threads to achieve the effects you want. What you choose will, of course, depend on the use to which you are putting your embroidery. Buttons would make a very uncomfortable cushion and you would not use feathers on a piece of work which you would need to wash!

'Penguins'. Group work (6-7) by Alwyn Infant School. Transparent plastic material makes convincing ice for this Antarctic scene.

'Self-portrait' by Toby Heaver (4 years 5 months). An old wig was used to give this self-portrait a realistic hairstyle.

Detail from 'Swans at Cookham'. Group work (9-10) by Holy Trinity Primary School, Cookham. The rims of yogurt pots and pipe cleaners have been couched down to make the bridge ornament. The pompom cygnets are in a nest of real straw. Frayed fabric suggests feathers on the swans' wing tips.

'Three-dimensional Landscape'. Group work (11-13) by Cox Green Comprehensive School. Macramé pins have been used for the telegraph poles and the real stones add both decoration and a contrast of texture to the smooth padded hessian fields and the fluffy pompom bushes. In the left-hand corner the vegetation is made of torn and painted foam, the river is a piece of fabric and the road on the right is sand sprinkled onto glue.

Finishing Your Work

When you have completed an embroidered panel, it should be stretched first (not ironed as it will be flattened by a hot iron) and then mounted.

How to stretch your embroidery

1 Lay five or six single sheets of newspaper over a drawing board (a). Cover the newspaper with a sheet of white blotting paper or thin white paper (b) to prevent the newsprint from coming off onto your work. Wet the paper until it is saturated but make sure there are no puddles of water lying on it.

2 Lay your embroidery (c) right side up onto the paper and pin it along one side with drawing pins *at the edge* of the fabric.

3 Pull the fabric very taut as you pin down the other side, working from the middle to the edges and making sure that the warp and the weft threads are kept straight. Pin the other two sides in the same way. Leave the work stretched on the board until it is quite dry and you are ready to mount it.

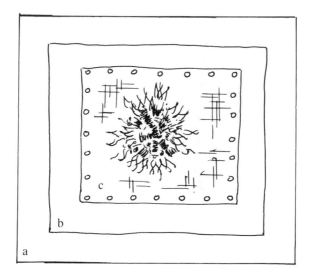

Stretching embroidery.

60

How to mount your embroidery

Very firm card for small panels, or pieces of hardboard for large panels, must be cut to the correct size. Be careful, when deciding on the size of the finished piece, that there is not too wide a margin of unembroidered fabric around your design.

Lay your embroidery right side down on a flat surface and place the board in position over it. Bring the edges up over the board and hold them in place with pins. Using a strong nylon knitting yarn, fasten the thread securely at the centre of one side and start lacing from side to side, pulling firmly as you work from the middle to the edges. Continue in this way until all the fabric sides are laced together across the board. It is important to fasten the thread very well each time you finish one thread and start a new one.

You can sew small rings on either side on the back about a quarter of the way down from the top and thread string through them from which to hang your picture. You might prefer to have it framed.

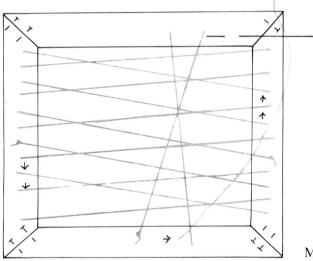

Mounting embroidery.

Useful Books

Starting points

Jan Beaney   *Fun With Collage* (Kaye & Ward)
                                  Fun With Embroidery (Kaye & Ward)
                                  Buildings: in picture, collage and design (Pelham Books)
                                  Landscape: in picture, collage and design (Pelham Books)
                                  Textures: in picture, collage and design (Pelham Books)
                                  Embroidery: New Approaches (Pelham Books)

Constance Howard   *Inspiration for Embroidery* (Batsford)
Jan Messent   *Embroidery and Nature* (Batsford)
Kathleen Whyte   *Design in Embroidery* (Batsford)

Stitches

Jan Beaney   *Stitches: New Approaches* (Batsford)
Anne Butler   *The Batsford Encyclopaedia of Embroidery Stitches*
                                  50 Canvas Embroidery Stitches (Coats Sewing Group)
                                  100 Embroidery Stitches (J. & P. Coats)
                                  Stitchery (Search Press)

Techniques

Jennifer Gray   *Machine Embroidery: Technique and Design* (Batsford)

Diana Springall   *Canvas Embroidery* (Batsford)
Mary Thomas   *Mary Thomas's Embroidery Book* (Hodder & Stoughton)
                                  Appliqué (Search Press)

Colour

Constance Howard   *Embroidery and Colour* (Batsford)
Johannes Itten   *The Elements of Colour* (Van Nostrand Reinhold)
Harald Mante   *Colour Design in Photography* (Van Nostrand Reinhold)

Creatures

Jan Messent   *Embroidery and Animals* (Batsford)
Barbara Snook   *The Zoo* (Batsford)

People

Valerie Campbell-Harding   *Faces and Figures in Embroidery* (Batsford)

Three-dimensional embroidery

Hannah Frew   *Three-Dimensional Embroidery* (Van Nostrand
                      Reinhold)
                    Cloth Sculpture (Search Press)

Printing

Harvey Daniels and   *Simple Printmaking with Children* (Van Nostrand
   Silvie Turner   Reinhold)
Mary Newland and
   Carol Walklin   *Printing and Embroidery* (Batsford)

Index

Numbers in heavy type indicate the page on which the method of working a stitch or a technique is explained.